Lakeland Ghosts

by

Gerald Findler

DALESMAN BOOKS
1989

The Dalesman Publishing Company Ltd.,
Clapham (via Lancaster), LA2 8EB.
First Published 1969
(as Ghosts of the Lake Counties)
This abridged reprint 1989
© Gerald Findler 1969, 1975

ISBN: 0 85206 974 X

Printed and bound in Great Britain by
Peter Fretwell & Sons Ltd., Goulbourne Street, Keighley,
West Yorkshire BD21 1PZ.

Contents

Illustrations in the text specially drawn by E. Gower.

Dedicated to Bill and Ethel Wright for their encouragement and help with this volume.

Foreword

ONE finds various names for ghosts, spirits or apparitions. In Northumberland one hears of a "swat-" or "swarf", in other places it can be a "wauf", and along the English side of the Border the word "fetch" was often used. "Barguest" was a term generally used to denote any kind of ghostly visitant, but referred more particularly to a fearsome creation which was supposed to haunt the Lakeland fells and dales and make weird and horrible noises. But the most common name in the Lake Counties is the "boggle", and this is a Norse word sometimes equal to personification or Saint. In his book *Cumberland and Westmorland—Ancient and Modern* (1857) J. Sullivan writing of swarfs and boggles says: "Though it would be unsafe to declare the entire extinction of boggles, it is certain that they have sensibly declined. The boggles of the present day are scarcely more than ghosts of boggles."

Introduction

THE fault of the present age is not that we believe too much but that we believe too little. We may scoff or sneer at some person who has seen a ghost or some other uncanny apparition, or heard weird knockings or witnessed some unusual and unearthly happenings, but with the memories of the Roman, Saxon, Danish, Norman and Border warfare in the Lake Counties, it is natural that the people living in that area — saturated as it is with legendry of the bygone centuries — believe in anything supernatural and superstitious. The vision of St. Cuthbert mentioned by the venerable Bede, the vision of St. Bega, the vision of St. Herbert, of St. Kentigern, of St. Ninian, all who appeared according to ancient history in this area — not always as human beings — but as spectres, have had their effect down the ages on the minds of the people in the north-west corner of England.

Superstition is clearly out of place in a civilised scientific world, but in spite of electricity, nuclear power, the possibility of the people of this planet taking space travel for granted, and the great advance of modern research, there are many individuals who adhere to the theory that ghosts, boggles, fairies, gnomes and unearthly visions still exist. As Robert Anderson, the Cumberland Bard, said: "The Genii that haunt the romantic valleys, the hills, woods and rivers of Cumberland and Westmorland, are so mischievous and malevolent in their disposition, so terrific in their aspect, and hostile to the human race, that a person would be thought very regardless of his safety, were he to entrust himself at any late hour of the night in the neighbourhood of their haunts."

Times have certainly changed since Robert Anderson's day and, whether we believe in the supernatural or not, most of us like to read or hear about ghosts or anything supernatural — weirdness, clanking chains untouched by human hands, skull and crossbones, frightening spectres, wraithes, spooks and boggles. Most people link these uncanny spooks with churchyards as the burial places of the dead, yet rarely are ghosts seen there. A churchyard is of course hardly a place for any person to visit on a dark night, or if it is visited and some wraith appears the frightened visitor is too scared to tell any living soul about it, so it is never recorded. Castles are favourite haunts of ghosts

6

and there is hardly a castle in the Lake Counties that cannot boast of clanking chains, weird happenings such as pictures and furniture being moved by some superhuman power, or screams, cries and moans after the midnight hour when ghostly figures glide silently along the castle corridors and disappear through the oak-panelled walls.

For some unknown reasons such weird happenings are not seen or experienced by everybody, but only by a selected few and rarely by those who actually go ghost-hunting. One might say: "Yes! Only by those people who are highly strung or with a very vivid imagination." Yet so many well educated people profess they have experienced the sight of a ghost. Perhaps due to the advent of electric light and the modernisation of old castles and halls, some ghosts have found it necessary to disappear from their usual haunts and will appear in some other locality.

What of the modern mysterious spectre? I have recorded an unusual visitor to a military hospital in Carlisle while I was on duty during the first world war, and also of a most unusual story of a chess player told by a Kendal man during an interview on Border Television. Having witnessed a number of deaths during my army service, I sometimes wonder what visions quite a number of dying soldiers saw when with open arms they reached out for some invisible being just before they "breathed their last". So who am I to say that there is no such thing as a ghost, boggle, spectre or spook, call them what you will?

GERALD FINDLER.

1.   Haunted Halls and Castles

For oft, the rustic peasants tell,
In midnight's howling storm,
When dreary winter's reign, is seen
A furious rider's form.
And in his arms, attired in white,
A lady fair is borne,
And lo! he vanishes away
At the first dawn of morn.
                                                    — Anon.

The White Lady of Naworth Castle

A GHOST is believed to hover around the lovely stream washing the base of the rock on which stands Naworth Castle, near Brampton, Cumberland. A Lord Dacre of Naworth Castle, the story goes, fell in love with and seduced a good-looking girl of the neighbourhood, who only learned of his rank and treachery after bearing him a son. In despair she threw herself into Naworth stream. Next morning her body was discovered by Lord Dacre himself, his newly-wedded bride and the girl's mother, who cried out the following curse:

> *Oh cursed be the cruel hand*
> *That wrought this hour to me!*
> *May evil grim aye follow him*
> *Until the day he dee.*

Lord Dacre's only son was killed by a fall from a rocking horse three years after the death of his father, thus bringing to an end the male line of the Dacres of the North, events very naturally associated by tradition with the mother's curse. For years this lovely spot was shunned by the natives, who were afraid of meeting "The White Lady".

The White Lady of Blenkinsop Castle

IT is strange that another ghost resembling a "white lady" should haunt a nearby castle. This phantom female was associated with the castle of

9

Blenkinsop, two or three miles from Haltwhistle and the seat of an ancient family who gave the fortress its name. The legend says that a popular member of this family, young Bryan of Blenkinsop, had one besetting weakness — an inordinate love of wealth. On one occasion he was present at the wedding of a brother warrior with a lady of high rank and fortune, and one of the toasts was: "Bryan de Blenkinsop and his ladylove."

Jumping to his feet, the passionate young lord exclaimed: "Never shall that be till I meet a lady possessed of a chest of gold too heavy for ten men to carry into my castle!" Too late he realised that by this foolish remark he had betrayed his weakness to his neighbours, and feeling ashamed he left the barony and "sought a countrie ayont the ocean tide".

Years passed and he returned bringing with him a wife and a box of gold, which it took twelve men to carry into his castle. But his marriage was not a happy one, for his wife heard of his reply to the toast and discovered that her gold and not herself had been the attraction. Maddened by jealousy she concealed her wealth in a secret vault. This action resulted in a quarrel and Lord Blenkinsop left the castle never to enter it again. His wife waited and waited for his return, sitting by her castle gate. She died broken-hearted, and her "spirit" haunted the castle gates at certain intervals — waiting — waiting — waiting.

Muncaster Castle's Headless Ghost

A GHOST without a head was said to haunt Muncaster Castle. If the legend of Tom, the fool of Muncaster, is any guide to whom the headless spirit may be, then it must be connected with a poor carpenter who fell in love with Helwise, the daughter of Sir Ferdinand Pennington of Muncaster. As his daughter was promised in marriage to a Millom knight, the father was so mad with anger that he bribed Tom to murder the carpenter. This operation was duly carried out, and as proof Tom cut off his victim's head to show to his master.

Irton Hall

WHEN the fugitive, Henry IV, was fleeing to Cumberland from his Yorkist foe he sought asylum with the Irtons of Irton Hall. They refused the unfortunate monarch, and he had to spend the night in a large oak tree, hiding from his enemies before going on to the hospitality of Muncaster Castle. One room at Irton Hall is said to be haunted by a lady in black —Ann Lamplugh, wife of John Irton, who refused hospitality to his king.

Lowther Castle

SIR James Lowther, the first Lord Lonsdale, fell in love with a woman of no connection, and when she died Sir James was deeply distressed and mourned his beloved to his dying day. According to the records of a Mr. Sullivan, "Sir James was with great difficulty buried, for while the clergyman was praying over his remains his ghost nearly knocked the reverend gentleman from his pulpit". After the burial there were disturbances in the rooms and noises in the stables, and no man nor animal could rest. After many attempts a priest laid the ghost to rest for ever.

Greystoke Castle Ghost

A DISUSED room in the old tower was the favourite haunt of a ghost, said to be that of a guest who was hunting with Charles Howard, Duke of Norfolk. After an evening of merriment the guest retired to his room but by morning he had disappeared, although his bed had been slept in and his clothes were lying about. Diligent search was made for him without success. It was said that anyone sleeping in the room afterwards was greatly disturbed, even if they were unaware of the tragedy.

Another ghost at Greystoke was that of a monk who was once bricked up in an underground passage, which strangely enough led from the chapel in the castle grounds to the bedroom mentioned above. In past years residents of Greystoke Castle have heard knockings on the wall as if someone needed help.

Corby Castle

PERHAPS the best known apparition in the north-west of England is that of the "Radiant Boy" of Corby Castle. In fact hardly any writers of books on British ghosts have failed to include the "Radiant Boy" in their collection.

Corby Castle on the banks of the river Eden, a few miles from Carlisle, housed the Howards of Corby for several centuries. The "Radiant Boy" was a luminous apparition that made very rare visitations to the castle, and it was recorded that any member of the Howard family who saw the "Radiant Boy" would rise to great power, then afterwards die a violent death. The only proof of this so far as is known was that of Lord Castlereagh, who committed suicide in 1822.

Hawkesdale Hall Ghost

WHEN Hawkesdale Hall was put in order some years ago two rooms were found that had been shut up for a long time. In one of the rooms neighbours say a boy hung himself. A phantom boy with a lantern reputedly comes out of the front door of the Hall on Allhallows E'en, and walks straight into the river Caldew.

Tallentire Hall Ghost

FOR several generations there has been a ghost story connected with Tallentire Hall, near Cockermouth. The tale was of a treasure hidden in the tower, and the headless ghost of a murdered girl. Outside the window where the murder took place, on the damp earth and pavement below, a small red fungus known as "Ghost's Blood" was often seen, and always returned however carefully removed.

Naworth Castle

A CURSE of a witch — said to be from the spirit world was in the form of a prophecy, part of which has come true: "When a bull shall toll the Lanercost Bell, and a hare bring forth on Naworth's hearth stone, Lanercost shall fall, Naworth be burned down and Dalstone Church be washed away."

Both conditions have at different times been fulfilled, which is the reason why two of the three buildings have suffered the fate of the curse. Much of Lanercost Priory is now in ruins and a great part of Naworth was destroyed by fire in 1844. Dalston Church is the only one of the three which has so far escaped its doom.

2.   Ghosts of Towns and Villages

The ghost in man, the ghost that once was man
But cannot wholly free itself from Man,
Are calling to each other thro' a dawn
Stranger than earth has ever seen; the veil
Is rending, and the Voices of the day
Are heard across the Voices of the dark.
— Tennyson (The Ring) 1889.

Caldbeck Ghosts

THE birthplace of the famous hunter, John Peel, at Caldbeck can boast of three supernatural happenings. Several years ago the local Women's Institute members compiled the history of Caldbeck which was edited by Dr. Mabel Baker and praised for its high standards by the adjudicator, Lady Dorothy Henley. These reports were made about hauntings:- Bushay House: A light was seen in the garden at midnight, for which there is no explanation; The Rectory: One room in the rectory facing the churchyard is said to be haunted by a chained ghost; the ghost is not seen, but the rattling of chains is heard.

Brigham Hangman's Ghost

AT Brigham the Carlisle hangman, Joseph Wilson, was buried in November, 1757. The sculptor embellished the headstone with the hangman's rope, but souvenir hunters chipped bits off until it disappeared. It was said that Wilson threw himself from the Cocker Bridge at Cockermouth into the icy waters below, evidently sick of his job. His ghost apparently haunted the Brigham churchyard until 1860, when the gravedigger unreathed Wilson's skull, packed it up secretly and delivered it to the house where the hangman used to live. The house was then occupied by two cloggers named Watson. After their deaths a mysterious wooden box was found in an old carved cupboard; you can guess the contents!

13

Martindale Boggle

THIS is well-known as the Henhow Boggle. In 1834 a man who saw the boggle was living in a cottage called Henlow in Martindale. His wife had heard some unaccountable noise in or around the house on various nights and informed her husband, but no further notice was taken. One morning, however, he had to go to work at an early hour, and having several miles to walk he started soon after midnight. He had not gone very far from the house, perhaps only 20 yards, when the dog at his side gave signs of alarm. He looked round, and at the other side of the wall that bounded the road a woman appeared carrying a baby in her arms. She kept pace with him as he hurried in his step in fear. There was no means of escape, so he spoke to the apparition and asked "what was troubling her". Then she told him her story:

She had once lived at Henshaw and had been seduced. Her seducer, to cloak his guilt and her frailty, met her by appointment at a certain market town and gave her medicine, the purpose of which was obvious. It proved too potent and killed both the mother and her new-born child. Her doom was to wander thus for a hundred years, forty of which had expired. On his return home the man told his wife of his uncanny experience and the story spread through the dale, one very old lady recalling the almost forgotten incident. The seducer was known to be a clergyman, who disappeared from the district immediately after the woman and her child had died.

This story was published in 1857 by J. Sullivan.

Thirlmere

AT Thirlmere a murder is said to have been committed in a house which was later destroyed. At this particular spot people have reported that a ghostly apparition in the form of a house with lighted windows appears from time to time. One wonders if the ghostlike travellers still call at the place where the *Nag's Head Inn* used to stand near to Thirlmere before it was closed to the public by Manchester Corporation. A friend of mine suggested that the ghostly visitors have travelled south and now call at the offices of the Corporation.

Egremont Pony Rider

WHAT is Christmas without a ghost? For in the Tarpot district of Egremont a ghost only appears on Christmas Eve. Legend has it that way back in the Middle Ages a fell farmer left an Egremont tavern on a stormy Christmas Eve to ride his pony back to his lonely farmhouse where he lived alone. Having imbibed to his full capacity, he was given a rousing send-off by his friends — and neither he nor his pony was ever seen again. Certain Egremont people place great credence in the legend, and claim that their parents or grandparents have actually "seen" the ghostly rider on his pony on Christmas Eve.

Binsey Fell Devil

THERE'S an old weird story about an old church. There was once a very wicked man who lived in a village; in fact he was so bad that people called him the devil. One day an angel came to see him and said that unless he mended his ways he would be sent to Hell and would burn for evermore, and therefore he must build a church in a field between sundown and dawn. So the wicked man, afraid of his future, started to build the church with stones and rocks which were lying about. He wore a leather apron in which to carry the stones, but as he hadn't much time he built the steeple at the wrong end of the church where it is to this day for everyone to see. In his hurry to complete the work his apron string broke. The stones which he carried fell out, and they now form Binsey Fell. While stones falling from aprons of giants are common legends in different parts of Lakeland, years ago it was alleged that on misty nights the ghostly figure of an old man with his apron full of rock could be seen.

Binsey Fell Devil: "An angel . . . said that . . . he must build a church in a field between sundown and dawn. So the wicked man, afraid of his future, started to build."

The Orton Boggle

PERHAPS the abortive attempt made to get up the Orton Boggle during the middle of the last century in Westmorland is as striking a proof as need be given of the decline of this belief. One characteristic occurred among the stories that then became current in the country. It was said that a "Methodee Man" (Methodist preacher) was brought in to exorcise the boggle, thus assuming for "Methodee men" the power supposed at one time to belong exclusively to Catholic priests. But the Methodee exorcist on receiving a blow with his own hat on the back of his head very properly declined any further interference.

A Prince at Kendal

IN Kendal is an ancient inn *The Angel* which stands near the Town Hall. It was given its name because of a spectre which appeared in 1745. Bonnie Prince Charlie with his army had entered Kendal, and his Highlanders were busy raiding and robbing houses for anything they fancied. Several of the Scots visited an inn and found it deserted, for the innkeeper and his family had hidden away in fear. But in their hurry they had left a small child playing about the floor. One of the Scots was about to seize the child, when a wraith-like figure appeared and drove the invaders from the inn.

This is perhaps among the best known ghost stories of Lakeland.

Morland Ghost

IT is a curious fact that most places which are said to be haunted have in the dark past years been the scene of fearful tragedies, and down the centuries have acquired an evil reputation. In 1827 at a place called Skellow Warle, in the parish of Morland, eleven human skeletons were found. It is said that among the eleven some had been buried with gold rings around their wrists, and some with graven ornaments on their temples. Not long before this gruesome discovery was made that place had the reputation of being haunted; a man of dark complexion was often seen to glide from one point of the rock to another then silently disappear into the thin air.

Penrith Gibbet Hill

THERE is a stone on the Beacon Edge Road, Penrith, which is known as Gibbet Hill, and a ghostly spectre depicting a skeleton hanging from a gibbet has been seen from time to time. The place was the scene of a murder, a man named Nicholson, in 1766.

A butcher from Langwathby called Thomas Parker was returning home from Penrith market, and called at the *Cross Keyes Inn,* Carleton, for a drink. The landlord, who was his friend, noticed his drunken state and offered to see him home. His help was declined and the next day Parker's body was found in Langwathby Road; he had been brutally beaten to death. A man named Nicholson, Parker's godson, was apprehended on suspicion, found guilty at Carlisle Assizes, and condemned to be hung on the gibbet at the scene of his crime. This was carried out on August 31, 1767, and the body hung exposed until all that remained was the murderer's skeleton. One stormy night the gibbet blew down, and the people from Eden Hall gathered the bones, wrapped them in a winding sheet and buried them.

Highwayman's Screams

JOHN WHITFIELD of Cotehill was a notorious highwayman who terrified people travelling the roads in the north-west. Few dared to venture out if he was in the district after dark. One day however in 1768 he shot a man on horseback in broad daylight on the Penrith-Carlisle road; a boy saw him commit the crime and was the means of his identification and conviction. He was gibbeted alive at Barrock, and for several days hung in agony. His cries were heartrending until a mail coachman passing Barrock (on the A6 road) put him out of his misery by shooting him. For many years after his death people travelling on the road near where Whitfield was gibbeted, affirmed that at night they heard the screams and cries of a suffering man.

Miterdale Ghost

THE remote farm at the head of Miterdale was deserted and became a ruin after a gruesome murder took place in the early 1800s. The body of the murdered man was buried close to the *Nanny Horton Inn,* now also in ruins. The spot is believed to be haunted by the murdered man.

The Ghostly Baron of Keswick

IN former times a church or abbey was built on the Keswick road at Stainton. The fields on the site are still called by various names — Kirk Garth, Kirk Syke and Kirk Rigg — and at various times human bones have been disinterred from this ground. This religious edifice fell into the hands of a certain Baron of reckless violence who employed men to remove the ruins of the church in order to build a stately house worthy of a man of his wealth. One day he rode his horse to the site to survey the work in progress, using plenty of profane language on the workmen busy building. Then he rode in the direction of Penruddock, and gaining the summit of the rising ground he was looking back to admire his land when his horse fell under him and he broke his neck. The place is now called Baron's Hill, and during the last century a ghostly figure mounted on horseback has been seen on the summit of the hill on winter nights.

17

Skinburness Screams: "It was to Skinburness that many couples fled, and the boatmen were only too pleased to 'oblige' and convey the lovers across the dark and rough Solway to the Scottish coast."

Skinburness Screams

SKINBURNESS on the Solway has passed through many phases. In 1302 the harbour and town were destroyed by heavy seas, but in later years a village by the same name sprang up further inland. Legends tell of fishermen's nets being caught from time to time in what is thought to have been the remains of the old town.

In years gone by runaway weddings were quite common occurrences, parents doing their utmost to stop young lovers getting away to Gretna Green. As the main coach road was through Carlisle it was to Skinburness that many couples fled, and the boatmen were only too pleased to "oblige" and convey the lovers across the dark and rough Solway to the Scottish coast. Legend has it that one such couple, together with their boatman, were drowned in a raging storm. Since that tragic ending the screams of the drowning couple have been heard coming from the Solway when it is a wild and stormy night.

Ambroth House

THE well-known artist and writer, W. T. Palmer, states in his book *The English Lakes* (1905): "Ambroth House is the haunt of the grisliest set of phantoms the Lake Country holds. For once a year, on All Hallowe'en, it is said the ghosts of the Lake Country, the fugitive spirits whose bodies were destroyed in unavenged crime come here. Bodies without heads, the skulls of Calgarth with no bodies, a phantom arm which possesses no other member, and many a weird shape beside. But they are a moral lot of victims and not sinners. Does the wild shriek in which ere dawning ends their banquet mean that to the spirit eyes has come a revelation of their wrongers in torment? But I forget; no man can hear that cry and live. Yet people will not believe the straight forward story of the Ambroth ghosts, of windows lit up with corpse-lights, of clanking chains in corridors, of eternal shriekings which cannot be traced, as though murder was being done in some secret chamber. But why has this house been compelled to be a ghosts' haunt? I have never heard a word against its reputation, ancient or modern. Perhaps it is most central for guests to the ghost supper."

A few youths who are students at Carlisle Grammar School have formed a club to go out ghost hunting in the Lake District. I suggest that All Hallowe'en eve spent in the vicinity of Ambroth House could possibly be an adventure they would never forget, that is if the annual conference of ghosts is still held.

Mass Murderer of Threlkeld

PERHAPS the most horrid crime of the Lake Counties was that committed by Thomas Lancaster of Threlkeld in 1671. Using white arsenic, he poisoned his wife, her father and her three sisters, her aunt, her cousin and a servant boy, besides giving poison to several of his neighbours who became seriously ill. He was found guilty at Lancaster and committed to his own house at Hye-Wrey to be hung from his own door until he was dead, and then taken by horse and cart to the Coulthouse meadows there to be hung up in iron chains on a gibbet at Sawrey Casey. The ghostly image of Lancaster hanging from the gibbet was seen quite often at night for many years.

Calgarth Hall Skulls

THERE is hardly a book written on English ghosts that does not include the story of the Calgarth skulls. Calgarth Hall, the mansion of the Philipsons, was reputed to be haunted for the misdeeds of a Naboth. His desire was to obtain possession of land belonging to an elderly couple, but they refused to sell and so he had them convicted of theft. The old woman, who in her way could be classed as a witch, pronounced seven curses against the Philipsons before the unfortunate old couple were hanged at Appleby. By some unseen power their two skulls returned mysteriously to Calgarth Hall. People employed on the estate were ordered to get rid of these hideous skulls, and tried to dispose of them without success. They were buried in the mountains, thrown several times into the lake and even calcined with lime, but the skulls always returned to Calgarth Hall. Each evening weird sounds were heard — groanings, shrieks and moanings — so finally to save further trouble the skulls were bricked into one of the thick walls, and then most people forgot about their existence.

Egremont's Haunted Tannery

ABOUT twenty years ago much interest was aroused in West Cumberland over a ghost which haunted an old tannery at Beck Green. An ex-sergeant of the police affirmed that his son, with three other young men, came from a garage opposite the tannery in a highly-strung and nervous state, and his son told him that they had seen a ghost. The police sergeant, with others, went to investigate and near the tannery observed what looked like a white mist rising from the ground. It gradually assumed the shape of a human body about five feet six inches in height, but there was no head and no feet.

Gradually the spectre floated down the road until it was opposite the entrance of the tannery; then a smaller ghostly figure joined it and both went into the tannery passing through the door. The women who were with the party were terrified, and another man who was with the police sergeant threw stones at the spectre but they went right through it. Many people at the time scoffed at this report of a ghost, and suggested it was caused by methane vapour rising from old mine workings, but the nine people testified that it was something inhuman.

Windermere

SEVERAL people from Windermere, writing to *Cumbria,* have occasionally heard strange roaring or howling sounds. One lady who lived in Windermere in 1895, when the whole of the lake froze, said that every night she hear loud and continuous moaning sounds coming from the lake. Experts state the noise came from the wind roaring through the cracked ice, but who can say?

Hugh Laithes Pike

HUGH Laithes Pike stands at the Burne Bank end of Haweswater, and is said to be the last resting place of a great sportsman named Jimmie Lowther. Unfortunately he was a great drinker as well, and when out steeplechasing while under the influence of drink he was thrown from his horse and met an untimely death by breaking his neck. As he died instantly he could not make a death-bed repentance, and so became very restless in his grave. He haunted the village and the Lowther parson made every endeavour to "lay" the ghost, but failed in his attempts. The frightened people took the matter into their own hands, dug up his remains, buried them on the highest point of Naddle Forest and placed a stone there to mark his grave. Where villagers were freed from Jimmie's ghost, people who have walked near the summit of Hugh Laithes Pike at dusk have seen a weird figure wandering around the stone.

Shap Giant

UTHER Pendragon, father of King Arthur, was a giant both cruel and cannibalistic. According to the legend, he occupied his time in trying to divert the river Eden so that it would form a moat for his castle. It has been stated that travellers going over Shap on wintry nights have seen in the distance a ghostly figure of a giant mounted on a mighty horse galloping at a tremendous speed. Perhaps it is Uther Pendragon who can find no peace, or maybe some other giant historians know nothing about.

Stainmore Headless Woman

A WILD district like Stainmore has for generations had its apparitions and its strange and weird noises. Perhaps the most well known is the headless woman, who even a few years ago was said to have been seen by lorry drivers on rough wintry nights. I can only repeat the story as recorded by Edmund Bogg in 1898, when he wrote the well known book *A Thousand Miles Wandering Along the Roman Wall:*

"A Saxon chieftain dwelt in a rude fortress on the edge of Stainmoor, acknowledging no king as his master, and between him and Fitz-Barnard, the Norman — whose stronghold was by the rushing Tees — was a bitter hatred, perhaps from the natural antipathy between the two races or possibly the right of chase on the moor which both claimed as their own. Be that as it may, the two parties had more than once come to blows while hunting, and in one encounter several retainers and the daughter of Fitz-Barnard, a beautiful girl of some twenty summers, were taken prisoners.

"The object of the chieftain was to make her his wife, and she was treated with all courtesy possible in that rude age. All his attempts to win her love were, however, fruitless and after remaining a prisoner for some time, she was rescued by stratagem, and was being borne triumphantly across the moor, when the Saxon appeared on the scene with a number of retainers and charged madly into the group of rescuers who were unable to withstand the onslaught, and the chieftain, furious at the thought of losing his fair captive, with one savage stroke severed the head of the young Norman from her body. Hence it is the headless woman seen galloping at midnight over the moor."

Cartmel Fell

THERE is a sad story told of the charcoal burners of Cartmel Fell. On two farms lived families who were about to be connected by marriage. The young male lover was a charcoal burner, and one day when watching his fire as he sat on a stone near his hut, he was struck dead by lightning. His pretty sweetheart, Kitty Dawson, went to his hut immediately after his funeral and would never leave it again. She sat hour by hour on the stone where her lover had sat when he met his doom, and continually called out his name. Neighbours cared for her by bringing her food and warm blankets, though they did not intrude. One day during the cold winter some men called with provisions, but as she made no appearance they entered the hut — and found her dead. People passing the spot have seen the ghostly figure of a young maiden sitting on a stone, and a woman's voice calling a man's name has been heard.

Brackenby Moor

DURING the first world war when I was convalescent at Red House, Appleby, I escorted a young lady home near the golf course at Brackenby Moor. After supper the young lady's father told me the moor was haunted. At one time there had been a murder on the moor, and since then people had seen ghosts, flames and other manifestations near where the murderer used to live. An ex-soldier friend of mine, who for a couple of months during the last war was stationed at Brackenby Moor, told me that quite a number of his friends had seen a ghostly figure near Moorland Tarn.

Gates Water

GATES Water by Coniston Old Man has quite a few weird stories. Down the ages people have spoken of pigmies and giants, of fairies and a host of evil spirits who moan and wail over shapeless mounds of rock, said to be ruins of cities of uncouth days. Today one can hear the call of the curlew and see a fox or otter, but perhaps in the darkness of the night other uncanny noises and weird shapes may appear for anyone with sufficient courage to find out.

Carlisle Ghosts

AN ancient city such as Carlisle must certainly have its share of haunted buildings. The castle is said to be haunted, as are the cathedral and the friary. A ghost was said to travel along a tunnel from the cathedral to the *Friars' Tavern,* but no unearthly sound or knockings have been heard since the tunnel was closed and, during various excavations along English Street, partially filled in. One cannot find any records or stories attached to such ghosts, and yet even today people living or working in the area of the original city claim that they have heard uncanny noises, which they assume come from ghosts.

Simon's Nick Ghosts

SWIRL How is the name of a mountain called by A. H. Griffin the "Queen of Coniston Fells". One side faces Westmorland down the lonely trough of Greenburn, and on the other side one looks over Wrynose to Cumberland. Yet Swirl How is in Lancashire and takes only second place to Coniston Old Man as the highest point in the country. Swirl How is little known in history, except for the miners of the middle ages who worked at the copper mines called Simon's Nick. They were named after a certain Simon who struck a rich vein of copper ore and told his fellow miners how the fairies had guided him to the spot, although some said the devil himself had been his guide. Time and again Simon's working was robbed until one day Simon was blown to pieces by his own gunpowder, either by his own choice, or by accident. It has been stated by climbers that Simon's Nick is haunted by the spirit of Simon.

Botcherby's Miserly Ghost: "Margery Jackson . . . wore an old long cloak, clogs on her feet, and hobbled about with the aid of a stick. Children called her a witch."

Botcherby's Miserly Ghost

BEFORE Carlisle Corporation built its rows and rows of council houses Botcherby was a pretty old-world village. My late father-in-law, with his wife and family of young children, lived in a large farm cottage at the top of the hill which was subsequently demolished and replaced by a grocery store.

The cottage, I was often told, was haunted by a miserly old woman, whose name was Margery Jackson and who died in February 1812. She wore an old long cloak, clogs on her feet, and hobbled about with aid of a stick. Children called her a witch, no doubt because of her long beard that grew on her wizened face. Her food was meagre, usually scraps of meat or bread picked up from around the stalls that stood in Carlisle's market place. A poor, starved woman, people thought, yet when she died she left over £50,000. Perhaps her ghostly figure still haunts the district where she lived, searching no doubt for some odd sovereigns she had hidden away and then forgotten. It is only about ten years ago since a tenant in a nearby council house complained that her house was haunted.

Keswick Road: " 'I heard galloping hoofs coming along the road . . . To my amazement—although the noise grew in volume—nothing appeared.' "

3.　　　　　　　　　　Haunted Highways

Still in the vision of the night,
We seem to see in fancies flight
Ghostly figures clear as day;
And then they vanish out of sight
In some mysterious way.

Keswick Road

ABOUT thirty years ago the following letter appeared in a Newcastle paper:
"While I was relieving the district nurse a number of years ago, I was called out at midnight to attend a case in a lonely cottage on the main road to Keswick. I was cycling along the road when the oil lamp on my bicycle went out. I dismounted and was fumbling for a match to relight the lamp, when I heard galloping hoofs coming along the road. I lit the lamp in a hurry thinking some cattle had strayed and might bump into me in the dark.

"To my amazement — although the noise grew in volume — nothing appeared within the radius of my lamp, which was shining down the road. A wind blew strongly against me and I could hear cartwheels as well as galloping hoofs. There was a strong impression of sweating horses and road dust, and then the sound gradually disappeared in the distance. I afterwards heard the tragic story of an elopement when the irate parent followed the runaway couple and shot the young man".

The Capon Tree Spirits

ON the roadside near Brampton there is a stone monument erected through the exertions of interested people to mark the site of the "Capon Tree", an ancient oak said by Hutchinson to have derived its name from the capons with which the judges and their retinue on their way from Carlisle to Newcastle formerly regaled themselves under its shade. Tradition also marks this as the tree upon which were hanged six of the rebels condemned to die for their share in the "Forty-five". "Six others", wrote Lieutenant-General Howard, the Governor of Carlisle Castle, "suffered last Tuesday at Brampton". The "Tragedy of the Capon Tree" records that "the spirits of the rebels were to be seen flitting about with airy ropes about their necks on each anniversary of the day of the execution."

Bassenthwaite

A PARTY of young people decided to climb Skiddaw to see the sun rise, and left Workington by trap about 10 p.m. to drive on their adventure. It was a beautiful moonlight night but while passing Bassenthwaite a hush suddenly fell upon the party for they all saw an apparition rising from the hedge. It rose until it reached human height, its deathly whiteness standing out against the darkness of the hillside, and then slowly made its way to the top of the hill where it stood a shining spectre. This strange apparition appeared at 1-30 a.m. and scared not only the party but also the horse which was pulling the trap. When the party returned to their home in Durham, two of the people found to their sorrow that a relative had died at 1-30 a.m. on that particular morning.

Gaythorn Hall

THERE is a story of a man who some years ago was passing Hollen Stump, near Ashby, on his way from Gaythorn Hall to Kendal Fair when he was very much alarmed by the apparition that suddenly crossed his path. He said that while walking along the road there galloped past him a ghostly figure without a head riding a white horse. On the headless man's shoulders was something like a flat board.

Winton's Jingling Annas

IT is said there used to be a wandering spirit between Winton and Kirkby Stephen of the name of Jingling Annas, which was laid to rest (exorcised) near the bridge crossing the Eden by the intervention of a wise man from Stainmore.

Ghosts at Reagill

IN 1910 I. S. Bland wrote of the hauntings of the ancient earthworks and mounds in Westmorland:

"Such is the case near Reagill Grange, where a gate noiselessly is opened for the midnight passenger, and again as noiselessly closed. At some other places a figure suddenly appears, passes by, and vanishes; sometimes a dog swelling into an enormous size; again a calf or black swine, and not infrequently a lady in white, whose antics are as various as her observers.

"This myth of the midnight air has often appeared to belated travellers, who, on daring her, have fallen victims to her fury. Major White of Reagill, one night coming through Blinbeck on horseback, saw something white in a tree, which he supposed to be a howlet. Having a gun with him he fired at it. With this salute it began to swell, and grew bigger till it took the form of a lady in white. She jumped on the horse behind him, and galloped behind him through the hedge, ditch, and brake at a terrible speed. At last he landed home, his clothes torn to shreds and his horse panting and white with foam."

Ghosts at Reagill: " 'Major White of Reagill, one night coming through Blinbeck on horseback, saw something white in a tree . . . It began to swell, and grew bigger until it took the form of a lady in white. She jumped on the horse behind him.' "

Lowther Castle's Ghostly Coach

A NATIVE of Lowther, the village near Lowther Castle which was the home of the Lords Lonsdale for many years, said that his grandfather often told him of a ghostly coach which was drawn by four wild horses madly rushing along the road towards Penrith. The coach was supposed to have carried the spirit of one of the Lords Lonsdale. As this was told to me personally, I have tried to trace a printed record of such an apparition without success. It may be a story concocted by an old man, or like other spectres in this book it could have happened.

Plumpton Mystery

ON the other side of Penrith, on the A6 road near to the village of Plumpton, is a spot where Toplis, the man who murdered a London taxi-driver was finally shot by a police constable. It may be a strange coincidence, but at this part of the road where Toplis met his doom quite a number of fatal motor accidents have occurred. People living near the place believe that some uncanny force is at work, which for one split second blinds certain car drivers at night.

A boggle's been seen wi twae heeds
(Lord help us!) ayont Wully car'us,
Wi twae saucer een and a tail;
They du say it's auld Jobby Barras.
  — Robert Anderson,
    "Nichol the Newsmonger."

Churchyard Vigil: "The old men of the parish would keep vigil at the church porch after dark, so they could be forewarned as to who would die during the ensuing twelve months."

Churchyard Vigil

APRIL 24 is the eve of the feast of St. Mark, and it was on this date over 100 years ago that a most gruesome custom was carried out in Cumberland and the northern counties. The old men of the parish would keep vigil at the church porch after dark, so they could be forewarned as to who would die during the ensuing twelve months. A Rev. W. Close recorded the following:

"In olden days it was a common belief that if you went into your churchyard between 11 p.m. and 1 a.m. on St. Mark's eve you would see pass before you the spirits of friends and neighbours who would die before St. Mark's day a year hence. It was a morbid watch, but one generally adopted."

Brocket, who wrote in 1829 of Northumberland and Cumberland customs, says that the spirits of those who are to die within a year of each St. Mark's eve pass through the porch of their parish church in their usual dress.

Uncanny Sounds

A LETTER, sent by a lady from East Yorkshire, appeared in a northern newspaper a hundred odd years ago. She related how she had spent a few days' holiday at Blindcrake, in West Cumberland, in an old world cottage:

"One night, for some unknown reason, I was unable to sleep, so I lit the candle intending to read, when suddenly I heard the sounds of soft music and beautiful singing, which seemed to come from the room beneath the one I was in. Then there was a noise as if forms or chairs were being moved, and the soft pad, pad of feet. Next morning I spoke of my experience to my host. I was told that beneath my bedroom was the site of a former chapel, where the monks sang and prayed hundreds of years ago, and that singing had occupied the room."

Piel Wyke Mystery

THERE is a peculiar story attached to Piel Wyke at Bassenthwaite, close to the *Pheasant Inn*. A family named Watson lived near Piel Wyke, and the children used to play on the fort which was then known as Castle Hill. One day the boys were digging at the side of the hill when they uncovered a hut with a slate roof and were quite excited as boys can be with their discovery. They were called away for their mid-day meal and afterwards rushed back to exploit their find, but were sorely disappointed when they could not find the place. Their spades were still lying where they had left them, but the hole was covered with grass.

The story could have been one of childish imagination but some weight was given to the truth of the boys' experience by their father, who a few days later saw two tiny people dressed in green on the level top of the Wyke. He set his dog on these uncanny creatures but some unknown power stopped the dog which came back to his master in a nervous state. The little green men disappeared into the ground and were never seen again.

Piel Wyke Mystery: "Their father . . . saw two tiny people dressed in green on the level top of the Wyke. He set his dog on these uncanny creatures, but some unknown power stopped the dog."

Arlecdon Mystery

EVIL spirits are blamed for the delay in the building of a church in what was known as Jackson's Park, Arlecdon. As often as the work was begun in the daytime it was destroyed during the night by some unknown force or invisible hand despite a watch being kept during the dark hours by men who said they neither heard nor saw anyone. Eventually the workmen got so scared that the work was abandoned, and the church built in its present positon. There are several quotations of spirits destroying at night the work of builders during the daytime. The Devil's Bridge at Kirkby Lonsdale is an example, but I prefer the legend that the Devil himself built the bridge and did not destroy it.

Ghostly Voices on Seat Sandal

A FEW years ago Miss M. K. Attenborough of Ulverston wrote the following letter to *Cumbria,* the popular Lakeland magazine:

"On August 1, 1949, my friend and I were ascending the steep grassy slope of Seat Sandal. We had left Dollywaggon by the wire fence and were keeping quite close to the fence all the time. Ahead of us, but out of sight we heard two men talking. There was a dog with them which we heard also, and from

30

time to time one of the men whistled as though directing the dog to sheep. We took it that we would see the two shepherds when we got to the top. At the top, the countryside was laid open before us for miles around, and there was not a single soul in sight, nor was there a dog.

"We made a thorough search without any results. Neither was there anyone on Grisedale pass, which we could see below. Possibly this was some trick of the ether and the two men and their dog were probably in an adjoining valley. Yet we seemed so close behind them that we could almost, but not quite, make out what they were saying. It would have been about 3-30 p.m. and it was clear and warm and sunny after a morning of mist and drizzle."

Great Broughton Mystery

ABOVE the banks of the Derwent there was once the St. Lawrence Chapel, and its site was visible to all because no matter what crop was grown in the large field which contained the outline of the graveyard, the churchyard itself was never ploughed. The Broughton people will tell you that it could not be ploughed. Horses reared up or dug in their hoofs when there was a sign of touching the sacred ground. But now the tractor, which is an insensible "animal", has been at work and the church ground has since been ploughed.

The "Death Light"

IT was considered in West Cumberland that a blue glow "death light" appeared as the spirit passed out of the body and would traverse the road the funeral followed. Several old people say their grandparents told them of such lights being visible on visiting houses where death had occurred.

The Mustard Mill

AT Skinrith Bridge, near Kirkby Stephen, a cleft in the rock offers a mystery; a subterranean noise may be heard by any person who applies his ear to the opening. It is recorded that this strange rumbling sound which issues from the rock is produced by the devil, who deep down there in the place below keeps his spirits continually employed grinding mustard. No one has ever known or even considered as to what happens to all this mustard, unless of course the devil likes mustard with every meal.

Fiend's Fell

THE highest point of the Pennine hills was once the abode of evil spirits, and for this reason was called "Fiend's Fell". A Christian missionary who chanced to come this way boldly ascended the mountain, exorcised the fiends, and erected a cross on the summit. Thus it got its present name of

Cross Fell. As the Helm Wind would at one time give an air of credibility to the legend, it is interesting to note that a story existed within the last century that a man and a horse and cart were carried away during a sudden severe storm and were never seen again.

Nab Ferry

SEVERAL ghost stories are connected with Nab Ferry, and the most sinister is that of an awful voice which on wild nights called out "Boat! Boat!" Whilst most boatmen ignored the call, more in fear than anything else, one bold ferryman answered the call, put off in his boat and rowed off in the darkness. Half an hour later he returned without a passenger, but he was terrified and was so shocked he could not speak a word. The next morning he was dead.

From that day stories were circulated of demons carrying off their spoils, of witched souls, and even bodies of dead saints, all being rowed across the lake. A priest came from Holy Golme, and with a bell and a copy of the Holy Bible he raised the skulking demon. For its peace, the priest laid the evil ghost in the depths of Claife, there to remain until "dryshod men walk on Winander and trot their ponies through solid crags".

Jacobite Story: " 'The woman awoke, and donning her cloak and bonnet, proceeded to the part of the wall pointed out by the stranger, and sure enough she found a key.' "

Jacobite Story

AMONG some old papers found in West Cumberland was the report of a ghost story connected with John Wesley, who was a great believer in haunted houses, apparitions and crystal gazing. The following story was related to Wesley at Ambleside:

"A Jacobite, who had taken part in the Rebellion of 1745, was tried at Carlisle and duly sentenced to be shot. On the evening preceding the day of his execution, his wife was sitting down at home and fell asleep. In a most realistic dream a stranger appeared to her and said 'Go to a certain part of the wall, and among some stones you will find a key which you must take to your husband.' The good wife awoke, and dismissed the dream as idle. It was not long, however, until she again fell asleep, and dreamed the same thing. The woman awoke, and donning her cloak and bonnet, proceeded to the part of the wall pointed out by the stranger, and sure enough she found a key. She asked for, and obtained, permission to see her husband for the last time, and managed to put him in possession of the key without being observed by the gaolers. According to the story, the key opened both the door of the cell and the lock of the prison gate, so that night at midnight the prisoner made his escape."

There is evidently some doubt as to the validity of this story which was told to Wesley, for the 1745 rebels were not shot but were hung by one William Stout of Hexham. Quoting Allan Cunningham: "We were told in our youth by an old lady who, when a girl, was present at the executions of some of the rebels at Carlisle, that most of them (all fine young men) were not half dead when cut down from the scaffold. One of them actually struggled with the wretch who opened his bosom to pluck out his heart."

Here is the awful sentence that was passed on the rebels: "You and every one of the prisoners at the bar, return to the prison from whence you came, and from thence you must be drawn to the place of execution; when you come there you must be hanged by the neck, but not until you are dead, for you must be cut down alive; then your bowels must be taken out and burned before your faces; your hands must be severed from your bodies and your bodies each divided into four quarters, and these must be at the King's disposal; and God have mercy on your souls."

What an end for an unhappy wretch!

Santon Bridge

A FEW years ago some young men from the Outward Bound School at Eskdale decided to camp out above Wastwater near Santon Bridge. During the night they were awakened by weird noises like dogs barking, geese gabbling and hysterical laughs of a woman. It was moonlight, and the campers got up and searched along the roads but there was nothing in sight. The place in which they were camping was too remote for anyone to play tricks, so they put the whole affair down as something supernatural.

Codale Tarn

PERCHED high up on a ledge is a small tarn with the name "Codale". It is six hundred feet higher than the neighbouring Easedale Tarn, and is classed by some as a small pool among the rocks. Many weird things are spoken of concerning Codale Tarn. One finds that through the mist climbers have seen the distraught face of a lost soul. The well-known Lakeland artist W. T. Palmer reported that in this region he had seen visions with grey beards, so clear and so true, that once he hailed a comrade whose face he saw, though his friend was forty miles away.

Death Customs

LAKELANDERS have had various customs concerning dead people. The popular one is to cover up all mirrors in the house where the dead person is lying as the spirit of the corpse hovers about the house for a period, and it is considered unlucky for those in the household if the spirit sees itself reflected in the glass. Some people who went to see the departed person touched the flesh of the corpse and then carried their hand to their own flesh. If they felt the touch cold they were intensely dismayed because they firmly believed they would die within twelve months. On other occasions, salt was placed on the corpse for various reasons, one being that the devil did not like his meat with salt on it. It is pleasing to note that such customs died a natural death.

Dobbies of the Fells

THE little folk of Ireland — the Leprechauns — are perhaps better known than the brownies of Scotland, but outside the north-west one seldom hears of the Dobbies of Lakeland. Yet some of the older inhabitants still talk of a family's own "Dobbie." For the Dobbie, a kind of household fairy, was once a regular resident of Cumberland and Westmorland. His habits were nearly the same as those of both the Brownie and the Leprechaun.

Only to favoured families did the little Dobbie attach himself, and the conditions of his service were simple — a bowl of milk and an oaten cake — or for a change of menu — a bowl of curds and cream — to be left every night for his use. In return he assisted the operations of the servants and assured his employers that all things would go well in the household. Any neglect of the Dobbie's simple demands was followed by the penalty of ill-luck in cooking, churning or cheese-making, and even the work of the day like weaving, knitting, sewing or washing was undone or spoilt during the night.

For some time no Dobbies have been seen in the Lake District, and the last records around 1850 concern Jack Wilson of Martindale. He was returning home in the moonlight and, nearing Sandwick Rigg, he noticed a large company of Dobbies intensely engaged in their favourite games. They observed him as he drew near, then climbed a little ladder into the sky. At the time of the construction of the Lancaster to Carlisle railway it was said that the Dobbies were angry at such a disturbance and started pulling down the big bridge at Shap. Perhaps with the modernisation of the roads the fairies or dobbies have, like many of the boggles and ghosts, deserted Lakleand for ever.

Ghost Army on Souter Fell

THE best authenticated story of all time is told, not of a solitary ghost or a large phantom dog or a mysterious coach being drawn by four fiery horses — no, none of these weird sights — but that of a full army of marching ghosts. In 1735, on Souter Fell near Saddleback, two farmworkers were astonished when they saw in the distance an army of men marching five abreast for a solid hour, each rank in turn disappearing over a sheer precipice. Very much afraid, after the phantom army had disappeared, they rushed away to tell of what they had seen. Their friends thought the two men had just had a little drop too much to drink because it was a very hot Midsummer's Eve.

But three years later the Souter Fell Army was seen again, not by the same two men but by thirty or more people. One man actually timed the first appearance of the soldiers until the final disppearance — and it took two hours. In the year 1745, ten years after the first appearance of the ghost army, hundreds of people witnessed this strange sight on Midsummer's Eve. So certain were some of the people present that they walked to the place where the army had passed to look for footprints but they found none.

It has been suggested that this was a "Brocken" spectre, formed of actual marching men on the clouds, but where was the real army at the time? Why would the same ghost army be seen at various intervals of years if it was a reflection? And why was such a spectre only seen on a Midsummer's Eve if it was a reflection of a live army?

Haunted Ships on the Solway

THERE are many stories of haunted ships on record, and the Solway is no exception for this type of phantom sailing craft. More than a century ago the *Rotterdam* sank in the Solway with all hands, and since then a vessel resembling her has been seen in the Solway — invariably before some maritime disaster. Elliott O'Donnell, the famous physic investigator, said: "Whatever the weather, the phantom *Rotterdam* pitches and rolls about, as if in the trough of a very rough sea. Ghostly figures are seen leaning over her sides, uttering from time to time the most heartending cries."

A ghost ship of a rather smaller size, supposed to be a phantom of a barque that was wrecked maliciously, also haunts the Solway. Is Mr. O'Donnell's ship, the *Rotterdam,* the same vessel as the one mentioned in the legend of the *Betsy Jane*? This was a slave ship which sank in the Solway near Whitehaven after returning loaded with a bright glittering gold and rare ivory, the reward for shipping load after load of wretched humanity in the form of negro slaves. The *Betsy Jane* was however only seen around Christmas time.

Haunted Ships on the Solway: " 'The phantom *Rotterdam* pitches and rolls about, as if in the trough of a very rough sea. Ghostly figures are seen leaning over her sides, uttering from time to time the most heartrending cries.' "

The Dunmail Warriors

IN my book *legends of the Lake Counties* I gave the legend of King Dunmail who, during a battle with Edgar the Saxon, was killed and buried beneath a pile of stones. Further to that legend it appears that the crown of Dunmail was charmed, giving to its wearer a succession to his kingdom. As King Dunmail lay dying he cried out: "My crown — bear it away; never let the Saxon flaunt it."

A few of Dunmail's stalwarts took the crown, fought their way through the

Saxon lines and consigned the crown to the depths of Grisedale Tarn, saying: "Till Dunmail come again to lead us." So every year the warriors come back to draw up the golden circlet from the depths of Grisedale Tarn and carry it back to the cairn of stones under which King Dunmail lies. They each knock with their spear on the topmost stone of the cairn and from beneath comes a voice saying: "Not yet, not yet; wait a while, my warriors."

5.　　　　　　　　　　　　　Animal Apparitions

The 'lated peasant shunned the dell,
For superstitions wont to tell,
Of many ghostly sound and sight
Scaring its path at the dead of night.

ANIMAL shapes are among those commonly assumed as "Boggles" —
large dogs, white horses, unaccountable cats and white rabbits. They are
said to appear in places where they have no business, to vanish through the
dark side of walls of stone, or to disappear down craggy steep paths near
which no well-meaning animal should be.

"'A farmer at Hackthorpe Hall was led to the discovery of
hidden treasure by the apparition in the form of a calf. He
noticed that the spectre always vanished beneath or near to a
large trough . . . and found beneath it a hoard of gold.'"

Last century the Rev. K. Simpson told the Kendal Natural History Society: "It is said that a farmer at Hackthorpe Hall was led to the discovery of hidden treasure by the apparition in the form of a calf. He noticed that the spectre always vanished beneath or near to a large trough, which at that time stood in the farmyard. He had the trough lifted on edge and found beneath it a hoard of gold, with which he afterwards purchased two estates in Cumberland. There is a somewhat similar story told of Howgill Castle."

The potters or gypsies of Lakeland had a good fund of "Boggle" stories of the animal sort which until early this century they related to each other around their camp fire at night. One daring potter ran after a huge weird dog, and ran and ran until it disappeared. But he took care never to do so again for this ghostly dog had led him to an old man who had committed suicide by hanging.

In the autumn of 1937 motor drivers going over Shap on the A6 road reported seeing a large dog racing in front of their cars for a few hundred yards and then taking a flying leap over a stone wall where there is a sheer drop of three hundred feet. It was only when several drivers related the same experience on different nights that they realised it was uncanny, for they had all seen the dog at exactly the same spot. An old roadmender now retired informed one of the drivers that this dog on Shap Pass is only seen prior to a motor accident when a person is killed.

Branthwaite's Phantom Dog

IN the Caldbeck district the Branthwaite Phantom Dog is nearly as popular as the famous hunter John Peel. One stretch of road at Caldbeck is haunted by a big black dog, an uncanny and frightening beast which appears from a holly bush in the hedge — and rushes along the road for some distance — before disappearing into another holly bush. It has been seen by several people.

Another phantom dog also appears in the Caldbeck district. A large black dog is seen occasionally, especially by members of a certain family, and someone is said to die the night following the appearance of the dog. It is quite possible these two phantom dogs are one and the same, and that we have two different versions.

The Burnmoor Ghost

WASDALE Head, from where coffins for burial were often carried on horseback across the moor, lends itself to ghostly stories. One tells of a coffin containing the remains of a young dalesman which was being carried over Burnmoor on horseback. Some invisible object suddenly frightened the animal which bolted into the mist and was unable to be found. When the tragic news was carried to his mother the shock of it gave her a heart attack, and within a few days she died. As her coffin was being conveyed over the moor, the horse carrying her remains bolted at the same place at which her son's coffin had disappeared. Diligent search was made, and the first horse with coffin was found. The second horse was never found. In the times of storm and mist a ghostly horse with a dark box-like shape on its back thunders past anyone alone on Burnmoor.

A Scared Potter: "He was awakened by the rattling of his stock of pots and pans so . . . he harnessed his horse and travelled seven miles to get away from the 'boggle.' "

A Scared Potter

HOW do a lot of ghost stories come to be told? There is the story of the potter who was travelling in Westmorland, and as night was coming on he pulled up at the road side, unharnessed the horse, and then crawled under his cart and settled down to sleep. During the night he was awakened by the rattling of his stock of pots and pans so he crawled out from beneath his cart and looked around. Seeing no one about he naturally thought the place was haunted, and therefore he harnessed his horse and travelled seven miles to get away from the "boggle". He stopped again to get some rest, but the pot rattling started again. As it was now daylight he looked among his wares and there was the secret — one of his potter friends, knowing of his habit of telling "ghost stories", had jokingly thrown a sack in his cart in which was tied a live cat.

Taylor Ghyll Force

CAN dogs sense anything that is supernatural? A friend of mine from Morecambe often walked down Taylor Ghyll Force in Borrowdale accompanied by his dog. Near a narrow gorge his dog would stop as if afraid, the hair on his back stiffening. My friend had to put the lead on the dog's collar and pull it along for some distance. Relating the peculiar behaviour of his dog an ex-policeman identified the spot as where a skeleton of a Liverpool man was found after being missing for fourteen months.

Weird Dogs

WESTMORLAND is supposed to be the favourite haunting ground for ghostly dogs, and if perchance the spectre of the dog is black then local superstition is that should the apparition follow you, someone near and dear to you will die. A large headless dog is said to haunt Eggholme, near to Kendal. Another headless dog once terrified people who had seen it round about midnight as it roamed near the watershed of Belah, and at times was seen between Milnthorpe and Beetham village.

Phantom ghosts of dog have also been seen at Crossthwaite, Lyth, Kirkby Lonsdale and Kirkby Stephen. A large mastiff haunts the Shap fells, and motorists report that they have seen it at night. The Kell-Bank Dobby is the name given to the ghost-dog that haunts the road between Lancaster and Kirkby Lonsdale. In her book *Guide to the Lakes* (1855) Miss Martineau mentions the ghostly figure of a large dog which can be seen swimming across Thirlmere.

Windermere

WHEN grievious trouble is about to happen a spectral white horse has been seen passing over the lake from shore to shore.

Ghostly Bat at Renwick

NORTH of the Penrith to Alston road is the village of Renwick, where the church dedicated to All Saints was rebuilt in 1733 and again in 1845. When workmen were pulling down the old church prior to re-building they were frightened away by a huge and hideous monster that resembled a bat-like bird and flew round and round the partly dismantled building. Believing it to be a vampire, the workmen rushed to their homes and barred the doors for fear of this "thing" attacking them. It is said that one man, braver than the rest, armed himself with a club made from a rowan tree branch, and after a fierce struggle destroyed the monster. But records show that since then, even as recently as ten years ago, people say they have seen an enormous black bird-like figure flying around Renwick on certain evenings.

Ghostly Bat at Renwick: "Workmen were . . . frightened away by a huge and hideous monster that resembled a bat-like bird and flew round and round."

6.   Recent Ghosts

Dim, peering through the vale of night,
Yon murky forms bring back a crowd,
Of images that seek the light;
That leap from out the misty shroud
Of ages — picturing as they glide
Athwart the tablet of my thought,
What did of good or ill betide
These walls, and all the deeds here wrought.
                                    — Anon.

IT appears that the modern ghost or spectre does not float about in thin air, clothed in a white sheet with arms outstretched, but comes fully clothed as a human being or becomes invisible when he performs some uncanny action. I have readers to decide whether the following reports, which have all appeared in the Press, are true or imaginary experiences of the persons concerned.

The Hospital Visitor

DO the modern ghosts appear as ordinary men and women? During the first war in the early part of 1917 I was serving with the R.A.M.C. For a period I was night orderly at an auxiliary war hospital in Carlisle. There were not many wounded Tommies in the hospital, and my duties were to see that they were comfortable during the night and to attend to their various wants. An Irish sister, Sister Cherry, was in charge and attended any of the Tommies needing special treatment.

In the playground, for the hospital was in a school, was a small wooden hut, and in it was an Australian sergeant with severe back wounds. By the light of an oil lamp I would go and read to him until he dropped off to sleep, then lowering the light I would return to the wards. One night as I walked across the playground to the hut I was surprised to see the lamp shining brightly through the window. I opened the door, and there by the bedside sat an oldish man holding Sgt. Chase's hand. I smiled and said I would come back later. Over a cup of tea I asked Sister Cherry who the man was who was with Sgt. Chase. She looked surprised: "Visitors at this time of night! Orderly — never!"

We both got up and crossed the schoolyard. As we neared the hut she

43

looked through the window and saw the man sitting with Sgt. Chase, but when she opened the door the light suddenly went out. "Light the lamp, orderly", she said. I obeyed but there was no one there — and Sgt. Chase was dead. The Sister and I laid him out, and she removed all his personal belongings as was her duty. In a wallet were several photographs, including one of the midnight visitor — the sergeant's father. There is a grave in Carlisle cemetery bearing the name Sgt. Chase. He was given a military funeral and the only two mourners were Sister Cherry and myself, but I felt the third although invisible mourner — the father — was with us.

The Hospital Visitor: "One night as I walked across the playground to the hut I was surprised to see the lamp shining brightly through the window."

The Ghostly Chess Player

DURING August of 1963, Mr. Peter Powell of Kendal was driving his car to Carlisle via Shap road when a man on the roadside thumbed a lift. As is natural when picking up a stranger, Mr. Powell asked the man what was his work. The passenger said he was a retired jeweller on his way home to Carlisle. They continued to talk on various subjects and then the

44

conversation turned to chess, which at first surprised Mr. Powell for although he was a keen chess player he had not mentioned the fact to his fellow traveller. The old man told him that now he was in his retirement he did nothing but compose chess problems. He had one which he had just completed, and said Mr. Powell must see it. On the outskirts of Carlisle the passenger asked him to stop at his home and invited him to come to the house, but Mr. Powell was in a hurry to get to the Border T.V. Studio where he was due to appear. He suggested that if it was convenient he would call back later. The man gave his name and address, and intimated that if he wasn't at home the chess problem was written on a sheet of paper and placed in his tobacco jar. At five o'clock that day Mr. Powell drove up to the house and asked to see Mr. ————. The woman who answered the door invited him in, but on hearing his story looked somewhat taken aback. "Can you describe him?" she queried.

The description was that of her husband. Puzzled she said: "That's strange, he died three days ago."

Mr. Powell noticed the alabaster tobacco jar on the mantelpiece and asked permission to open it, to which the widow agreed. Inside was the chess problem written on a sheet of paper just as his passenger had described. The tobacco jar and the sheet of paper were afterwards shown in the television programme on which Mr. Powell duly appeared.

In order not to distress the widow Mr. Powell would not divulge her name or address. Was this really an after-death manifestation? Or was it just an experience of one's imagination? Mr. Powell is an intelligent man with three sons, and certainly not the type of person to pull a fast one on the general public. No doubt in years to come this experience will be told and retold until it becomes "The Legend of the Ghostly Chess Player".

Carlisle Citadel Bar

DO ghosts like a drink? During 1959 the Press reported the case of a ghost in Yeldon, Bedfordshire, who on several occasions during the night when a public house was closed and all doors locked pulled himself four pints of beer and left them standing on the bar counter. The ghost figure at Carlisle must be a much better-mannered individual for he visited the *Citadel* bar before it was modernised in 1967, went up to the barmaid and ordered himself a bottle of beer. Then in full view of a few men in the bar he walked through a thick brick wall and disappeared without having his drink.

Hollow Stones' Ghost

IN his book *In Mountain Lakeland* the author A. H. Griffin mentions a well-known climber's experience during the first world war. One day the climber had been on Scafell Crag, and on the way down Hollow Stones during a lovely summer's afternoon he was joined by a very close friend, rather unexpectedly because he thought his friend was in France fighting. The two men talked about the times they would spend together when the war was over, and then parted and arranged to meet again in a few days. One day the climber received a letter from France telling him his friend had been killed in action on the very afternoon they had met each other on the way down Hollow Stones.

Ghost Lights

EVIDENTLY some ghosts are invisible but helpful. During January of 1969, the warning lights on the new eight-mile Penrith by-pass really baffled experts. The lights switched themselves on, and electronic experts stated: "They are designed to be switched on by a radar signal from a passing patrol car. But on a number of occasions the lights have switched themselves on." If a ghost is responsible he is certainly well acquainted with modern methods.

For Whom the Bell Tolls?

TO end this book on a humorous note, we are reminded when the church bell tolls its sad and solemn note at a funeral service that the custom arose from an ancient belief that the angels and devils fought for possession of the passing soul at the funeral. Evil spirits were thought to be afraid of the sound of bells, so that the louder they rang the better the soul's chance of reaching heaven. A Lakeland bell-ringer said at one funeral: "I'll not waste my time on't bells for Jos Netherington, I's not reely bothered which side gits the auld fule."